D0122189

Why Limit
HAPPY
to an
HOUR?

Why Limit HAPPY to an HOUR?

A Little Book of Wit
(and a Whole Lot of Attitude)

Mary Phillips

**Andrews McMeel
Publishing, LLC**
Kansas City · Sydney · London

10 11 12 13 14 SDB 10 9 8 7 6 5 4 3 2 1

ISBN-13: 978-0-7407-9748-4
ISBN-10: 0-7407-9748-4

Library of Congress Control Number: 2009943928

www.andrewsmcmeel.com

Art and text by Mary Phillips.
Graphics by Emily Morrison.

ATTENTION: SCHOOLS AND BUSINESSES
Andrews McMeel books are available at quantity discounts with bulk purchase for educational, business, or sales promotional use. For information, please write to: Special Sales Department, Andrews McMeel Publishing, LLC, 1130 Walnut Street, Kansas City, Missouri 64106.

Why Limit HAPPY to an HOUR?

"Delusions of grandeur make me feel a lot better about myself."

— Jane Wagner

Today's Agenda: Get through it.

TO DO

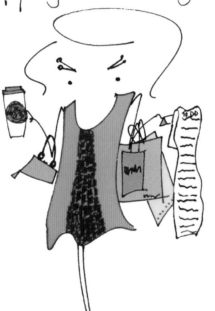

We're a drinking village with a fishing problem.

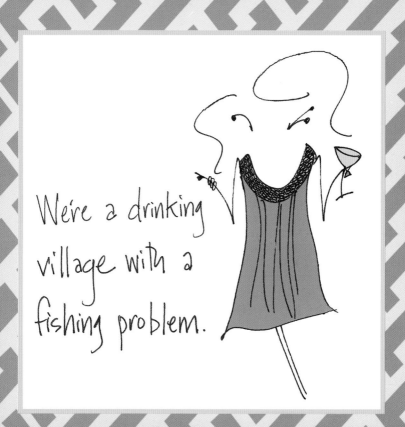

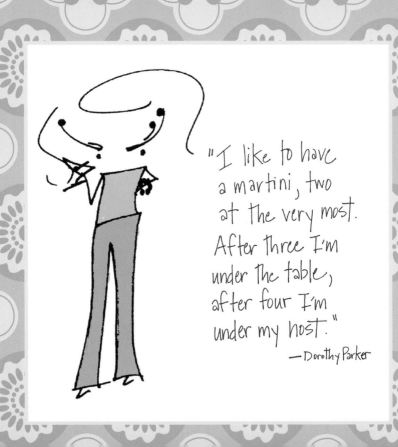

"I like to have a martini, two at the very most. After three I'm under the table, after four I'm under my host."

—Dorothy Parker

"I feel sorry for people who don't drink. When they wake up in the morning that's as good as they're going to feel all day."

— Frank Sinatra

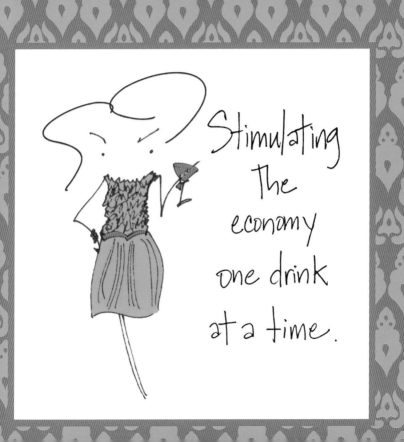

Stimulating the economy one drink at a time.

"Research tells us that 14 out of any 10 individuals like chocolate."

—Sandra Boynton

The nice part about living in a small town: When you don't know what you're doing, someone else always does.

There are two theories for arguing with women.
Neither one works.

If you've got it,
flaunt it;
and if you don't,
go out & buy it.

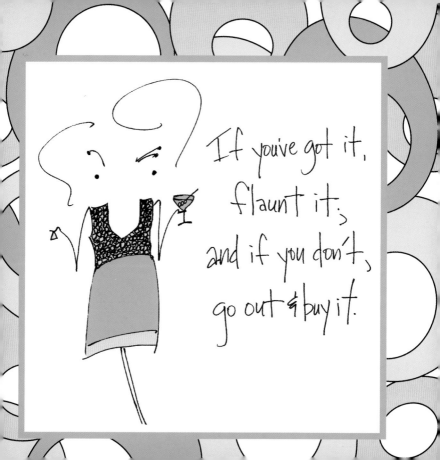

I want to be
Barbie—
that bitch
has everything

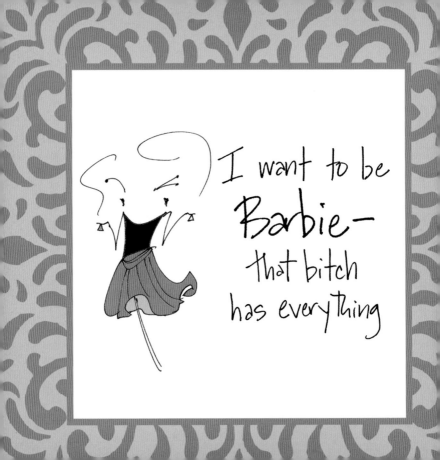

"I don't even butter my bread. I consider that cooking."

—Katherine Cebrian

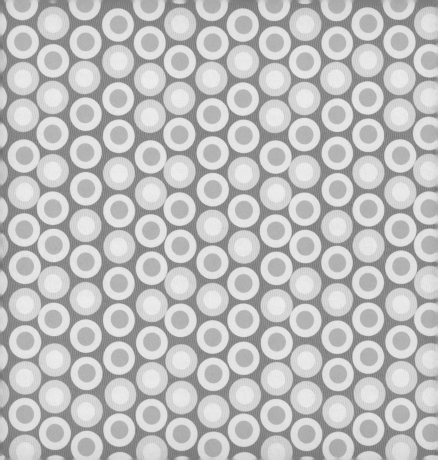

Why limit happy to an hour?

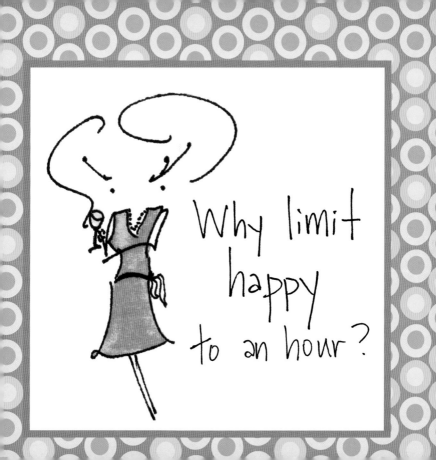

To Do
1. Ladies' Lunch
2. Garden Club
3. Baby Shower
4. Cocktail Party
Stop me before I volunteer again.

Put your big girl panties on & deal with it.

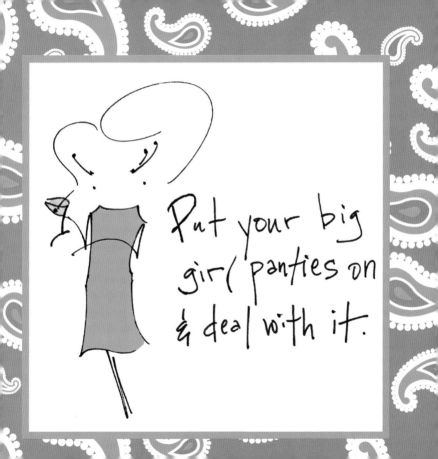

"I have high heels & low morals."
—K.T.G.

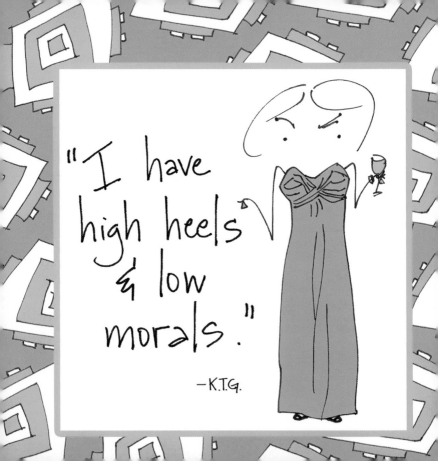

Never let a few facts stand in the way of a good story.

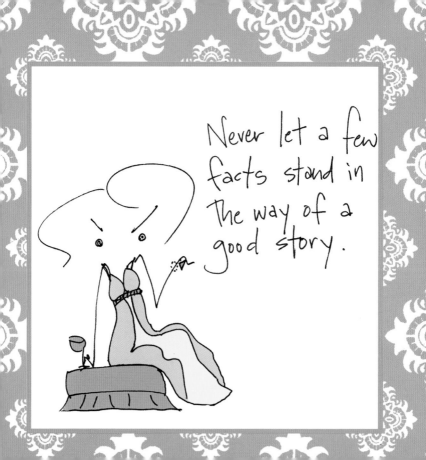

"I get a kick out of myself & that's all that matters."

— R. Lee

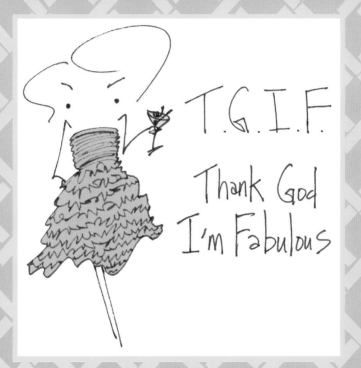

T.G.I.F

Thank God
I'm Fabulous

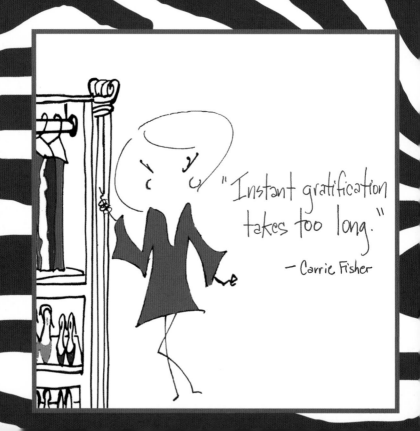

"Instant gratification takes too long."

— Carrie Fisher

Breakfast
is
poured.

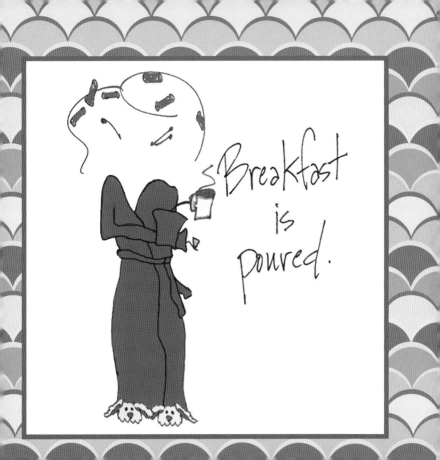

Wine flies when you're having fun.

"Happiness is good health and a bad memory." —Ingrid Bergman

To save time let's assume I know everyThing.

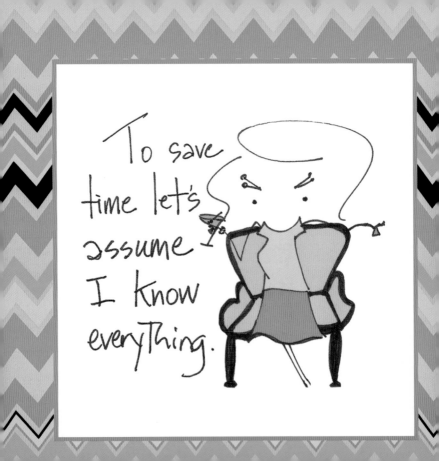

A balanced diet.

"If you obey all the rules, you'll miss all the fun."

— Katharine Hepburn

I'm not bossy, I just have better ideas.

Some call it cocktail hour;
for me it's a
support group.

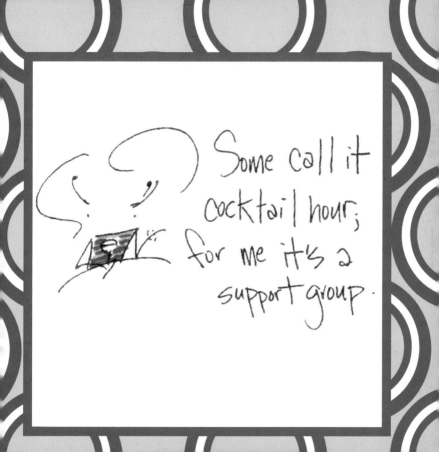

Save the earth— it's the only planet with wine.

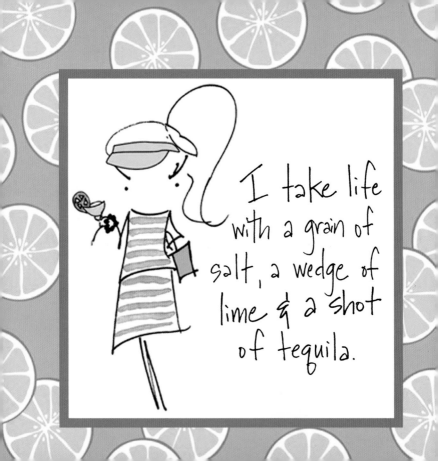

I take life with a grain of salt, a wedge of lime & a shot of tequila.

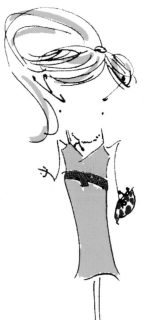

"I find low self-esteem incomprehensible. Why hate yourself when you can hate others?"

— Amy Ashton

Waiter, I'm going to need a bigger glass.

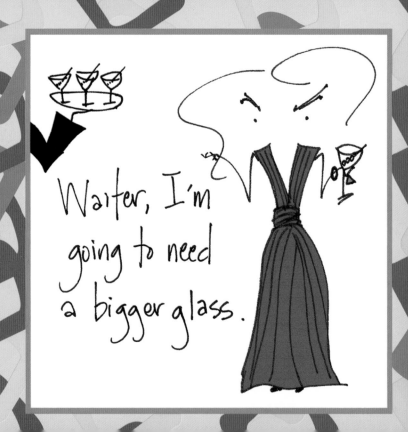

Countless numbers of people have eaten in This Kitchen and gone on to lead normal lives.

I know I'm in my own little world, but it's ok, they know me here.

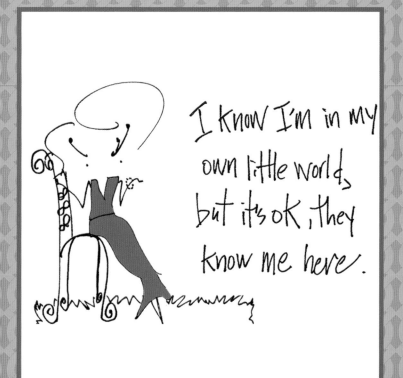

When life gives you lemons, add vodka.

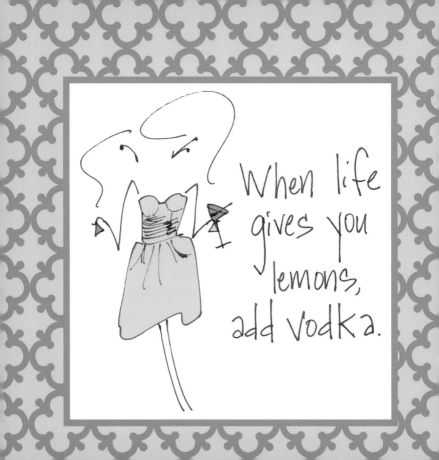

It's only a drinking problem if I'm sober.

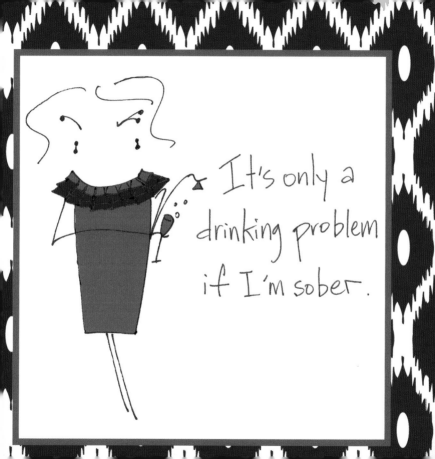

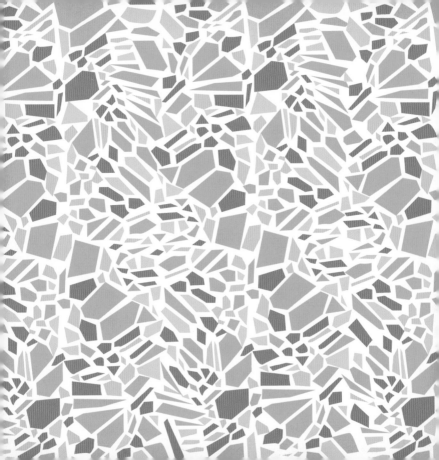

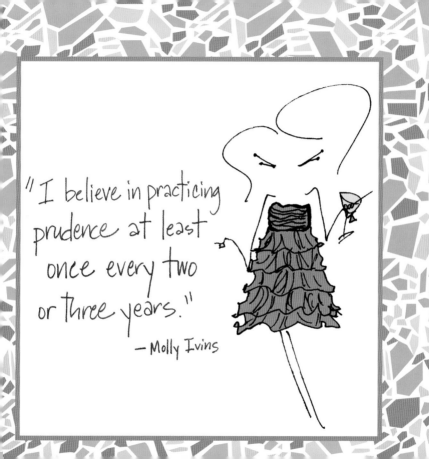

"I believe in practicing prudence at least once every two or three years."

— Molly Ivins

4:00... when 5:00 just won't do.

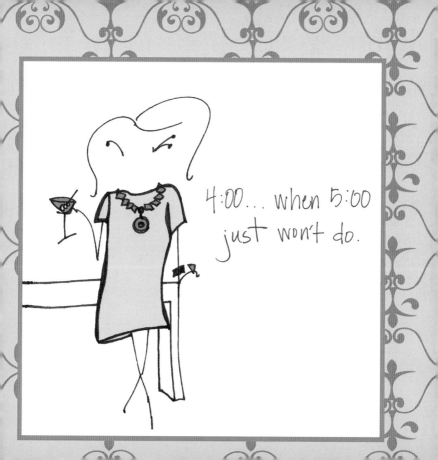

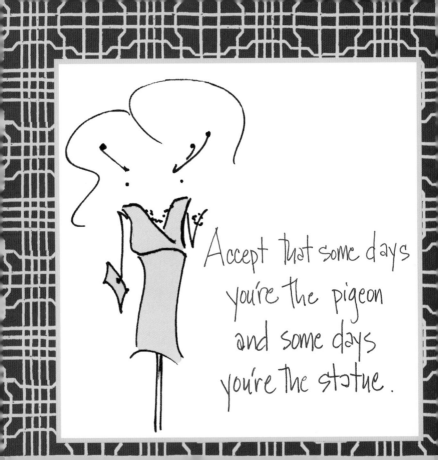

Accept that some days you're the pigeon and some days you're the statue.

It's 5:00
somewhere.

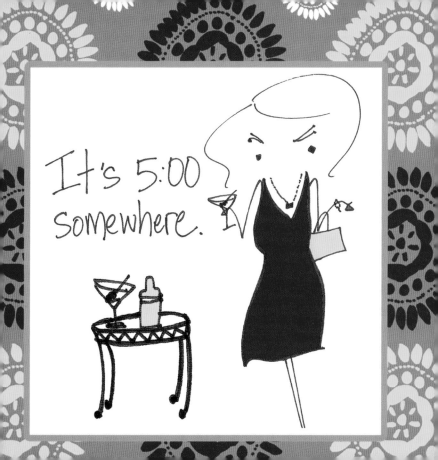

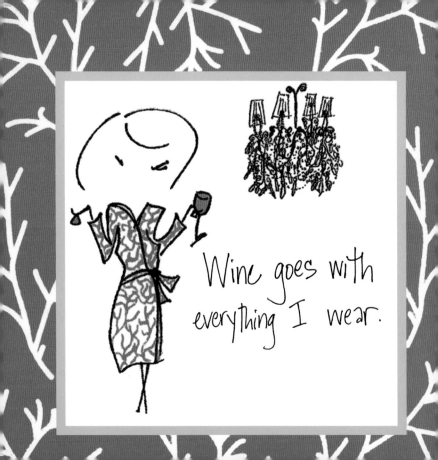

Wine goes with everything I wear.

I used to care but now I take a pill for that.

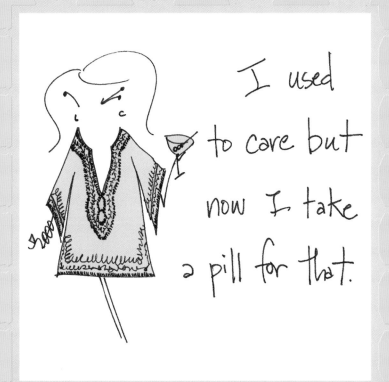

Inside me is a Thin woman screaming to get out... I can usually Keep The bitch quiet with chocolate.

You say potato;
I say vodka.

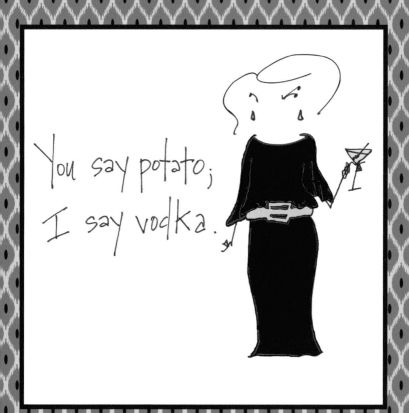

Domestic bliss is only a drink away.
JW

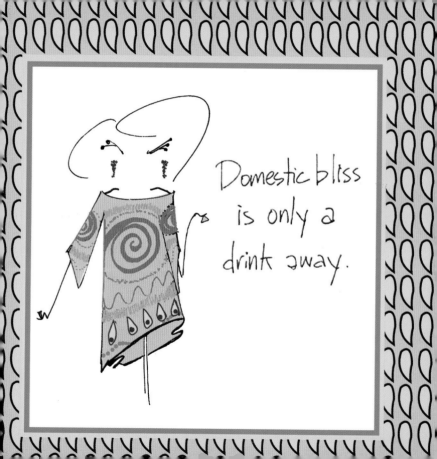